HUMAN ANATOMY
for Children

YOUR BODY AND HOW IT WORKS

by Ilse Goldsmith

Dover Publications, Inc., New York

Published in Canada by General Publishing Company, Ltd., 30 Lesmill Road, Don Mills, Toronto, Ontario.
Published in the United Kingdom by Constable and Company, Ltd.

This Dover edition, first published in 1969, is an unabridged and unaltered republication of the work originally published in 1964 under the title *Anatomy for Children*. The work is reprinted by special arrangement with Sterling Publishing Co., publisher of the original edition.

ACKNOWLEDGEMENT

The author wishes to thank Elbert Tokay, Associate Professor of Physiology at Vassar College, for his invaluable assistance in checking the illustrations.

Standard Book Number: 486-22355-8
Library of Congress Catalog Card Number: 78-85445

Manufactured in the United States of America
Dover Publications, Inc.
180 Varick Street
New York, N.Y. 10014

CONTENTS

I. The Human Body as a Machine

In many ways the human body can be said to resemble a machine; each performs work and each has specific parts that do particular jobs.

These specific parts work together to make the body function just as the various parts of a car work together to make it run. If one small part is injured or not working properly, the whole body may stop functioning. In a car, too, if one small wire is damaged or loose, the car may not be able to run.

Hair and skin protect the body, much as paint protects the automobile. The human bones form the skeleton or frame and support and shape the body, as the metal frame supports and shapes the car. Food serves as fuel for the body to give it "power," just as gasoline or petrol is fuel for the automobile. A car has a radiator and an exhaust, and so has a human being. But here the similarity ends, for nothing man-made can really come close to the almost perfect creation, the human being.

2. Cell Structure

Look into a mirror. What do you see? You see yourself as an individual human being, with the various characteristics that make you *you*, and not the boy or girl next door. Physically, you are really very much like everyone else. Each part of you, from the roots of your hair to the tips of your toes, is made up of individual microscopic cells. Different kinds of cells group together to form tissue, and tissues group together to form organs like the heart, lungs and stomach.

Each human cell has a thin wall around it to hold the cell material together. This wall is called the cell "membrane." This membrane is very flexible and can be pushed and squeezed into different shapes. Once the force that is doing the pushing or squeezing is removed, the cell membrane goes back to its original shape. The cell wall or membrane is also permeable (allows certain substances to pass through). Because of this permeability nourishment and waste material can enter or leave it.

Inside the cell wall is the material which makes up the largest part of the cell. It is called "cytoplasm." The word comes from two Greek words, *kytos*, which means "hollow vessel" and *plasma*, which means "form," or something "moulded." Cytoplasm is a watery jelly, much like raw egg white. In the middle of the cell is a small dark mass which is the nucleus of the cell. The nucleus like the whole cell also has a wall around it. (This wall is called the "nuclear membrane.") It is in the nucleus that all the functions controlling the cell take place. If the nucleus is removed, a cell will die. The only exception to that rule is the red blood cell about which you will read later (on page 76). The nucleus also contains the factors controlling heredity— the chromosomes and genes.

The cells of each tissue look somewhat different and have different functions because each tissue has a different function:

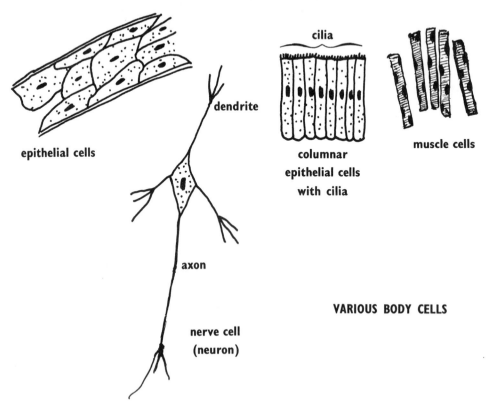

epithelial cells

cilia

columnar epithelial cells with cilia

muscle cells

dendrite

axon

nerve cell (neuron)

VARIOUS BODY CELLS

There are six main kinds of tissue in your body:

1. Skin and the covering of the insides of the mouth and digestive organs is called "epithelial" tissue.

2. Connective tissue; this holds the muscles together and keeps all the organs in place.

3. Blood tissue.

4. Muscle tissue.

5. Nervous tissue.

6. Gland tissue.

Facts about cells

Cells are made up of proteins, fats, sugars, and starch.

Cells contain small amounts of mineral salts, vitamins, and enzymes (digestive aids).

Some specific cells contain a great amount of one particular chemical; for example, red blood cells contain large quantities of iron, and bone cells contain large quantities of calcium.

The adult human body is made up of:

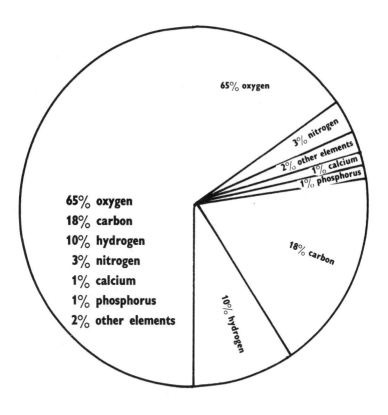

65% oxygen
18% carbon
10% hydrogen
3% nitrogen
1% calcium
1% phosphorus
2% other elements

3. Hair and Nails

Why do you have hair?

Man has developed as a hairy creature, and the hair on his head and body was originally for warmth and protection against the elements.

You can see that individual hairs do *not* grow in straight lines. Take a magnifying glass and look at a part of your arm. You will see that there is a pattern in the way the hair grows.

Hair is arranged in clusters much as scales overlap on a fish. The hair on your head or scalp grows the same way. There is a definite pattern to it, and that pattern is already there in a newborn baby. Look at a tiny infant when you can. You will notice a fine down all over his body. Later, as he grows, this down or fuzz will become hair. Because the skin covers a larger area as one grows, the hairs are further apart, and then they no longer look like downy fuzz.

What is normal hair growth?

There are approximately 1,000 hairs to each square inch of scalp.

You average about 120,000 hairs on your head.

Each hair has a life-span of 2-4 years.

Every day new hair grows and old hair falls out.

Each hair is always at a different stage in growth from the hair next to it.

The new hairs are lost among the older, longer strands.

Even the eyelashes follow this same pattern of growth.

Each eyelash lives about 150 days.

Your hair is much like a forest. When you look at a forest before entering, you see many tall, thick trees. It is not until you walk through the forest that you see old trees dying, new ones growing, little trees, big trees, medium-size trees. It is only when you examine your hair carefully that you can see the little new short hairs mixed in with the older, longer, thicker hairs.

What makes hair grow?

A hair starts to grow when the cells in the skin form a pocket which becomes the hair "follicle" or "sheath." The root of the hair (the only live part of the hair) is inside that pocket. New cells grow out from the root and push the older, dying cells up. The hair that you see, the strand, is just a long line of cells that have piled up. You can visualize this if you picture a tube of toothpaste. When you squeeze at one end of the tube a line of toothpaste comes out.

There is blood flowing to each hair follicle which feeds the individual

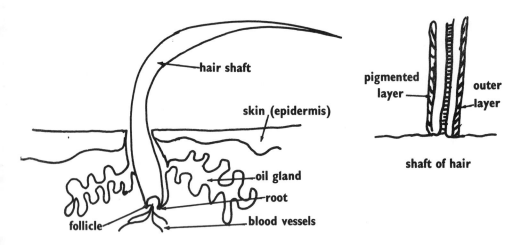

Labels in diagram:
- hair shaft
- skin (epidermis)
- oil gland
- root
- follicle
- blood vessels
- pigmented layer
- outer layer

shaft of hair

root. Oil glands empty oil into the follicle and the oil spills out over the hair. This oil keeps the hair lubricated, so that it does not become dry and brittle and break.

What makes hair fall out?

When the "papilla" (the connective tissue around the root of the hair) shrinks, it stops the nourishment flowing to the hair. The hair dies and falls out.

There are two types of baldness. One is caused by illness, high fever or emotional upsets. The hair falls out while the illness or upset lasts, but usually re-grows once the sickness is over.

Baldness is usually due to heredity. A man inherits the tendency to become bald from his parents, just as you inherit the color of your eyes. There is one main difference, however. Women rarely become totally bald, even if they inherit a gene for baldness from each parent. Men will become partly or completely bald if they inherit even one gene for baldness from their parents.

1 gene for baldness
1 gene for hair

Parents

1 gene for baldness
1 gene for hair

Both parents are carrying similar genes. The mother is not bald; the father is. If this couple had daughters they would not be bald. The sons this couple have could be bald or not depending on the genes they received from their parents.

Offspring

(1) 25% chance
2 genes for baldness
totally bald as an adult

(2) 25% chance
1 gene for baldness
1 gene for hair
partially bald as adult

(3) 25% chance
1 gene for baldness
1 gene for hair
partially bald as adult

(4) 25% chance
2 genes for hair
full head of hair as adult

Dandruff

Everyone has "dandruff." It is made up of the loose dead cells from the skin of the scalp, mixed sometimes with dried oil from the glands. The hair keeps these dead cells from washing or rubbing away as the dead cells do on the rest of your body.

Blonde, brunette or redhead?

Hair color, like eye color, is inherited. The pigment for color is deposited in cells of each new root and is found in the second layer of hair.

As a person grows older, pigment often is no longer made. Each new hair growing has no pigment and so it appears white.

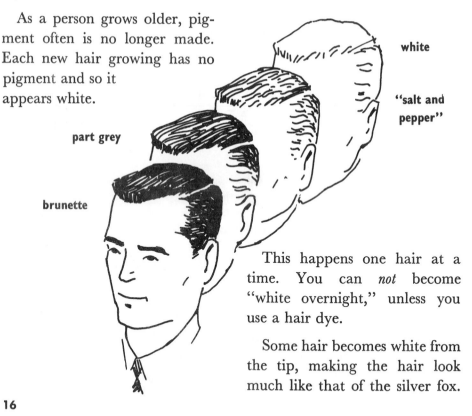

white

"salt and pepper"

part grey

brunette

This happens one hair at a time. You can *not* become "white overnight," unless you use a hair dye.

Some hair becomes white from the tip, making the hair look much like that of the silver fox.

Curly or straight?

You inherit this quality also from your parents. It depends on the shape of the individual hair. Each hair is round or flat. Straight hair is round. Curly hair is flat.

SINGLE CURLY HAIR   **SINGLE STRAIGHT HAIR**

Pull out a hair, and cut off the end with a sharp pair of scissors. Look at it under a microscope or magnifying glass. If hair has just the smallest wave to it, it will be a flat hair.

More people have curly hair than straight hair. Hair varies from straight to kinky. Orientals and North American Indians have completely straight hair. At the opposite extreme is the Negro, who has very curly or kinky hair.

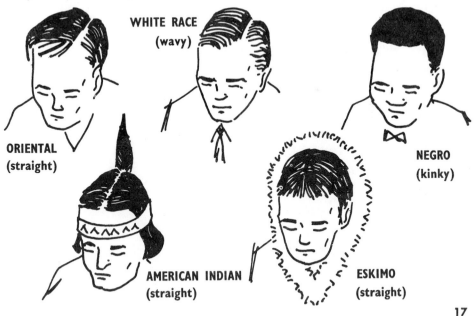

WHITE RACE
(wavy)

ORIENTAL
(straight)

NEGRO
(kinky)

AMERICAN INDIAN
(straight)

ESKIMO
(straight)

17

Nails

Just as the hair grew to protect man, the nails on the fingers and toes grew to protect those areas. Also like the hair, the nails are a special part of the skin, and are made up of hornlike skin cells. A baby, even before it is born, has special nail buds that become the nails just before birth.

Each nail has a root out of which the nail grows. The root of the nail is deep in the dermis layer of the skin and as the nail grows out it becomes thicker and thicker.

The nail at the root is attached to the bone in each finger and toe by connective tissue. You can get somewhat of a picture of the shape of the root because the white portion that looks like a half moon just above the cuticle grows parallel to the root. This white area is the softest part of the visible nail and is made up of newly made nail cells, and is easily cracked or marred.

If a nail is injured and has to be removed, it will grow back as long as the root of the nail is healthy and alive. However, once you injure and kill the root, the nail is gone. This happens very rarely. Often, though, you may see a nail that has part of it mis-shapen and different from the rest of the nail. This is a sign that part of the root of the nail is damaged.

The nails, like the hair and skin, do show signs of body health or disease. If all the twenty nails on the body have cracks or grooves running lengthwise, the doctor knows that something is physically wrong, perhaps anemia (a disease where there are too few red blood cells made by the body).

If there are these lengthwise disturbances on only one or a few nails, then this is a sign that only the roots of these nails have been affected, perhaps by a local infection of these roots.

Sometimes grooves or cracks run from side to side in the nails. The sideways disturbances show that something has upset the body only for a short time, like pneumonia or sea-sickness. Of course, if there are sideway cracks only on the fingernails, then perhaps the damage was caused by improper manicuring. These marks all grow out, however, and disappear after a time.

Facts about hair and nails

The only parts of the human body that are hairless are the palms of the hands and soles of the feet, undersides of the fingers, undersides of the toes, and the lips.

"Goose pimples" are caused by tiny muscle cells at the base of hair follicles. These muscles contract when you are very cold or frightened and you can see them then as little bumps or "goose pimples." When they contract, the hair also straightens up. In an animal, such as a cat, you can actually see the hair "stand up" on end.

If you completely remove a nail without injuring the root, it will take five to six months before the nail has grown back completely, because a nail grows approximately 1/25 of an inch per week.

It takes three to four weeks for a nail to grow out from the root until it becomes visible above the cuticle.

4. The Sense Organs

These organs are the eyes, nose, ears, taste buds and special nerve endings, causing sensations of feeling or touch in the skin. They are the teachers and detectives for the whole body. The nose, eyes and ears tell you all about the goings-on away from the body. The taste buds on the tongue and the nerve endings in the skin let you know what is happening to the body. With all your sense organs you learn about the world around you and your own surroundings.

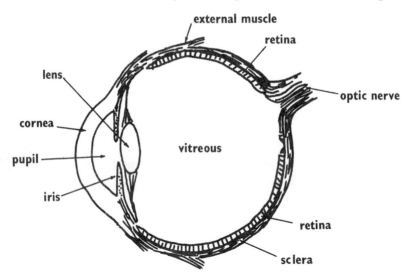

How do eyes help us to see?

Look out of a window at one object. Perhaps it is a tree. Light falls on the tree from the sun or in the dark, from a street light. The light

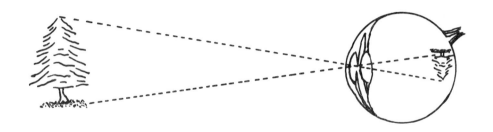

rays pass through the "transparent cornea," the "pupil," and the "lens." The lens bends these rays so that they strike "rods" and "cones" on the "retina." These rods and cones transfer the light rays into electrical impulses which travel along the optic nerve to the brain. The brain then decodes these impulses and you "see" the tree.

The pupil of the eye is just a hole in the middle of the "iris" (the colored section of the eye) that admits the proper amount of light into the eye. At night, or in a darker room, the pupil is larger. In

(1) Dimly lit room, the pupil tends to be somewhat enlarged

(2) Shining a flashlight directly at one eye you can see the pupil closing to pinpoint size

(3) In a dark room the pupil opening is very large

bright sunlight it becomes pin-point in size. You can see this change for yourself. All you need is a mirror and a good flashlight. Stand in front of the mirror with a flashlight in your hand. Turn out the lights in the room or pull the curtains, so that the room is relatively dark. Keep your eyes open. Hold the flashlight below one eye and turn it on. See what happens to the pupil.

What is 3-D vision or depth perception?

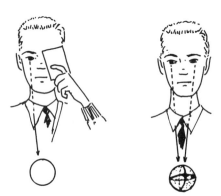

If eyes are used properly, both eyes see an image. The right eye transmits its image to the left side of the brain, the left eye to the right side of the brain. From these two pictures the brain forms one image. The slight difference in the images causes "three dimensional vision," or "depth perception."

It is this "phenomenon" that enables you to play ball games well and lets you judge with fair accuracy how far away a moving car is. Depth perception occurs only in man and higher animals such as the apes.

How do you see in the dark?

When you go from the street into a darkened theatre, at first you see almost nothing. In a few minutes you can barely see the outlines of the seats, then you can see which seats are occupied, and finally you can walk down the aisle and pick out a seat without being afraid of sitting on someone's lap.

22

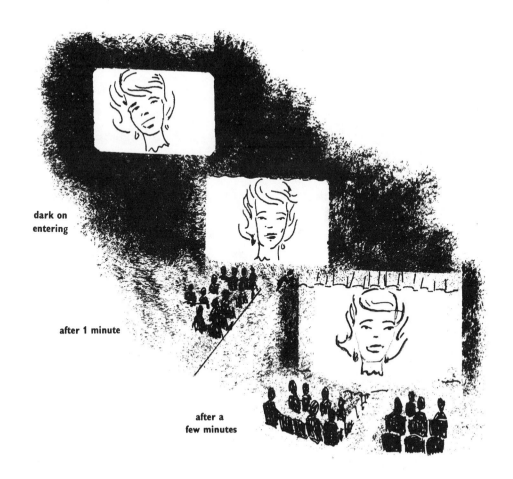

dark on
entering

after 1 minute

after a
few minutes

What causes this gradual ability to see?

The rods on the retina are sensitive to small amounts of light. As you go from the bright outside into the dark, the rods are becoming more and more sensitive, until, in about 20 minutes, you can see well, or rather you have become "dark adapted." For this reason, anyone planning on riding a bicycle at night should stay outside a few minutes, so that he becomes at least partially "dark adapted" before beginning to ride.

Facts about eyes

Blinking is a reflex action and each person has his own "normal blinking rate."

An infant does not blink regularly the first few months of its life.

The fluid that covers the eye is mostly tear fluid. By blinking, you actually draw this fluid over the eyes. The tear fluid does not spill over the lids because there is an oily secretion covering the lid edges. (That is why you put butter on a jug spout to prevent dripping.)

You cry tears when a nerve in the eye is stimulated. Sneezing and coughing stimulate this nerve. Emotions also can cause this nerve to be stimulated. Only human beings can cry when they are emotionally upset. Animals cry only when they sneeze or cough.

Tiny babies do not cry tears when they are upset until they are about five months old.

How do ears help us to hear?

A sound is made when movement occurs, setting up vibrations heard by the ear. These vibrations pass through the air in the form of sound waves. When these sound waves are picked up by the ear, you hear the sound. Everything has a sound of its own. There is the spoken sound, there is the sound of music, of water, of wind in the trees, or the sound of danger approaching, such as an automobile horn.

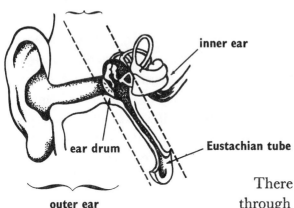

There are three main parts through which the sound wave must travel to be heard:

1. The outer ear.
2. The middle ear.
3. The inner ear.

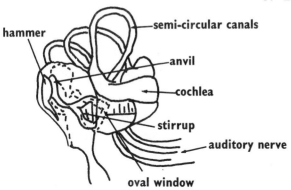

Between the middle ear and the outer ear is the "ear drum," which is a thin piece of skin about $\frac{1}{4}$-inch across. It works much like the skin stretched across a drum. When a sound wave hits the ear drum, it vibrates. This vibration is passed on to the "hammer" or "malleus," a small movable bone in the middle ear. The moving hammer hits

25

another bone, called the "anvil" or "incus." The anvil starts the third bone, the "stirrup" or "stapes" moving. These three bones are just transmitters of sound.

The sound wave is sent on to the inner ear by the flat bottom of the stirrup. This fits into an opening between the middle and inner ear called the "oval window." The movement of the stirrup in and out of the oval window is passed on to the watery fluid of the inner ear or "cochlea." It is called this because it looks like a snail's shell and "cochlea" comes from a Greek word which means snail.

The movement of the liquid inside the cochlea stimulates the nerve endings in the cochlea. At this stage a remarkable thing happens. The sound waves become converted to electrical impulses and travel from the cochlea along the "auditory nerve" to the brain. The brain interprets these electrical impulses as sound.

There are many sounds that are impossible for man to hear. In order to hear a sound, the vibration caused by that sound must be felt by the ear drum. If the sound does not vibrate enough to make the ear drum move then it is not loud enough to be heard by you. Sound not only travels through air, it can travel through water, wood

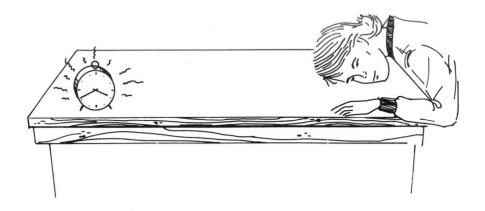

and many other materials. To prove this, all you need is a clock and a table. Put the clock on one end of the table, press your ear against the other side of the table and you can hear the clock tick.

Sound also travels along string; you can use this principle to make a walkie-talkie telephone. All you need are two tin cans and a long string. Punch a hole in the bottom of each tin can just large enough to run the string through and tie a knot. As you talk into your can, the sound makes the string vibrate and your voice can be heard in the other tin can held by your friend.

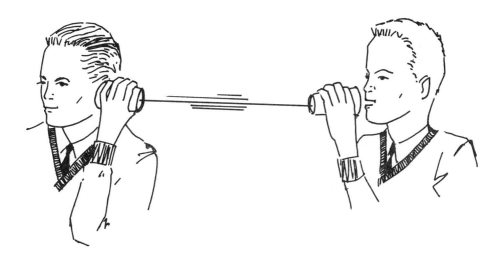

Beside hearing, the ears also perform another service: they help the body to maintain balance. This is done by the "semi-circular canals."

They are three hollow semi-circles, each of them filled with liquid. When you move, the liquid in these canals moves. This causes a change in pressure in the canals. Information about this pressure change is sent to the brain. When the brain has interpreted the message, it relays the information to the correct areas of the body which force you to balance yourself.

If you place yourself into a moving vehicle such as a boat or a plane, or even a roller-coaster, something else happens. The liquid in the semi-circular canals is constantly shifting as the boat, plane or roller-coaster moves, even if you remain quite still. The brain interprets these moves as your movement, and sends messages to the body to make up for this movement. It is this misinterpretation by the brain that may cause nausea, dizziness, or what is called "motion sickness." After a while, the brain does adjust to the situation, and no longer compensates for the movements not made by you. Then you have what the sailors call your "sea legs."

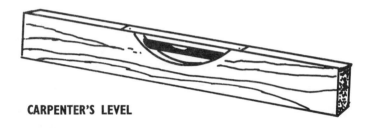

CARPENTER'S LEVEL

In a similar way, a carpenter uses a tool called a "level" to determine if a beam is balanced and straight. The level has a small bulb in it filled partially with water. In this bulb floats an air bubble. At the slightest change in position the air bubble shifts, and the carpenter knows that he must adjust his beam.

Facts about hearing

The speed of sound is slower than the speed of light. This is why you see lightning just before you hear the thunder.

Sound waves can be used to find objects many miles away. Radar and sonar make use of this fact.

The air carries many, many vibrations at the same time. If you could hear them all, the noises would be terrifying. Fortunately many noises cause vibrations beyond the range of the human ear.

Some sounds travelling at extremely high frequencies, called "ultrasonic waves," can be used to sterilize instruments, pasteurize milk and even drill teeth.

The nose

Smells are caused by chemicals in the form of gas in the air. Everything has its own special smell. Sometimes smells are just for pleasure, such as "woodsy" smells or "flowery" smells. Sometimes a smell can tell you of danger, for example, the smell of smoke, the smell of spoiled food or the smell of leaking gas. Some smells even help you to enjoy your food. That is why, when you have a cold and can not smell, many foods seem to lose their taste.

The nose has special cells in a certain area in the nasal cavity. When the gases in the air are breathed in, they are recognized by these cells. Once the cells have analyzed the gases and recognized the aroma, the cells send a message to the brain through the olfactory nerve and the brain records the smells.

The brain actually remembers smells. That is why a smell can often bring back a memory. For instance, if you once lived near a bakery, you often smelled that marvellous aroma of freshly-baked cakes and breads. If, after some time you pass a bakery and smell the aroma again, you will probably find yourself remembering many things about the old locale where you first smelled that aroma.

The nose also acts as a filter for the air you breathe. It keeps out dust and small particles in the air by using the little hairs in the nose as a trap. This way, the dirt particles do not reach your lungs.

The nose has still another function. It warms the air you inhale so that by the time the air reaches your lungs, it is at body temperature (98.4° to 98.6°F.).

Facts about the nose

By blowing your nose incorrectly you can cause trouble in your ears. There are two tubes from the middle ear that open in the upper part of the throat. They are "safety valves" to keep the air pressure in the middle ear the same as the outside air pressure. When you blow your nose and hold one nostril closed, back pressure develops and forces these tubes open. Then the germs and mucous you are trying to blow out of your nose are forced back through these tubes into the middle ear.

The tear fluid that covers the eye leaves the eye constantly when you blink, through a canal that goes into the nose. There it evaporates or runs out.

"Sinuses," the holes or hollows in the bones of the head all empty into the nose. When the nose is stuffed up due to a cold, these sinuses cannot drain and through being stuffed up can give you a sinus headache.

After a while, you become accustomed to smells, and you no longer smell them. This enables scientists to work with foul-smelling chemicals, and not be disturbed by the aroma. You can prove this. Blindfold a friend. Hold a piece of cheese with a sharp aroma under his nose for several minutes. See if he can tell you when you remove the cheese from under his nose.

What are taste buds?

These are special groups of cells mostly on the upper part of the tongue. They respond to the chemicals in food. Various parts of the tongue are sensitive to different kinds of taste; for instance, the front detects sweet and salt and the back, bitter tastes.

AREAS OF TONGUE SENSITIVE TO TASTE

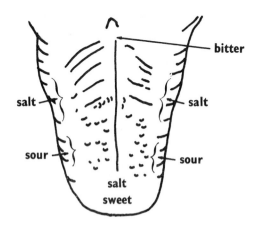

Sometimes what you think is taste is really smell. You can prove this very simply. All you need is an apple and a pear and a friend. Blindfold your friend, hold a pear under his nose and put a piece of apple in his mouth. He will think he is eating a pear.

How is the skin a sense organ?

It is sensitive to temperature, pain, pressure (touch). This is due to the nerve endings in the skin. In the skin there are more nerve endings that are sensitive to pain than there are deeper inside the body. This enables the skin to serve as a warning system.

Different areas in the skin have different types and numbers of nerve endings. The fingertips are especially rich in nerve endings. The skin on the hands and face has fewer nerve endings sensitive to heat and cold than the rest of the body. This enables you to leave your face and hands exposed when you go out in the winter and yet not feel the cold.

When you are testing the water in the bathtub with your hands, you may discover that the lack of nerve endings in the hands for temperature works against you. Your hands feel comfortable in the bath water and in you go. You then discover with dismay that the water is far too hot for comfort for the rest of your body.

Now you know why mothers test the bath water for babies with their elbows, which are far more sensitive to temperature changes than the hands. For the same reason they may test the temperature of a baby's formula on their wrists.

All the sense organs acting together are the detective agencies to help tell you about the world in which you live. Working together with reasoning and memory, the sense organs give you information about yourself and your environment.

The skin has other functions besides being a sense organ—it is the fortress of the human body. It protects the body from outside invaders like germs and bacteria; it prevents the fluid that feeds the cells from evaporating and it helps to keep the body temperature constant.

It is made up of layers very much like a package of sliced cheese. Through these layers, the blood vessels, hair and nerves grow.

The top section, or "epidermis" is made up of several layers of dead cells that are stretched out and flattened. These dead cells are brushed off daily, by washing and through clothing rubbing against the skin. There are no nerve endings in this layer of the skin and you can easily cut it and not feel pain. You can actually see these cells from this layer. Take a fingernail, run it over your arm, and clean it out on a microscope slide. Through your microscope you can see lots and lots of epidermis cells.

CROSS-SECTION OF SKIN

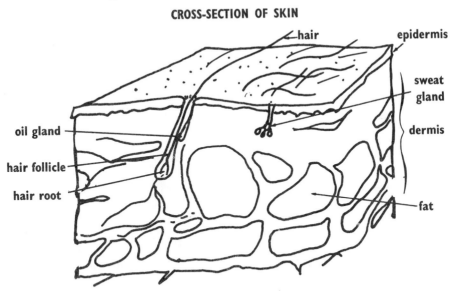

Underneath this layer is the "dermis" or factory. It is here that the oil is manufactured to keep the outer skin (epidermis) lubricated and flexible; otherwise it would crack and wrinkle. This oil comes from the gland around each hair follicle. It pours out and over the skin. You can see this oil. Take your finger and rub it over the area where your nose joins your cheek, then wipe that finger on a clean glass. See the oily streak.

As a man becomes older, this oil is not produced in such quantity and so the skin dries out and wrinkles. To demonstrate how this happens, all you need is some plain cooking oil, water and a sheet of paper. Cut the sheet of paper in half, and brush oil on one half only. Now wet both sheets and put them somewhere to dry. When the sheets are dry the one soaked in oil will be smooth. The one without the oil will be wrinkled.

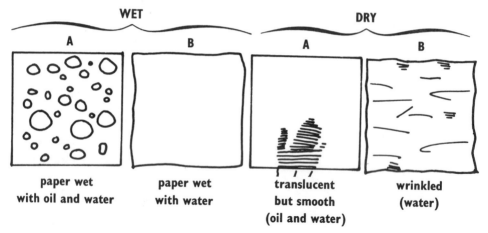

WET   DRY

A   B   A   B

paper wet with oil and water   paper wet with water   translucent but smooth (oil and water)   wrinkled (water)

How does the skin keep the body temperature steady?

You have pores or tiny holes all over your skin. When you are hot, these pores open and permit perspiration to pour out and evaporate. The evaporation cools off the body. When you are cold, the pores close very tightly and so there is no evaporation. These pores are very much like windows. You keep them open during the warm weather and close them when it is cold. You can test this yourself. Use some rubbing alcohol (being a spirit it evaporates more rapidly than water) and rub some on your wrist. As it evaporates you can feel your wrist becoming cooler. This is why an alcohol rub can bring down a high fever.

As perspiration evaporates, it leaves salts and other waste materials on the skin. These wastes and dead cells and dirt in the air collect on the skin. The skin oils hold all these materials. This is why you should take a warm bath or shower to really become clean. It not only makes you feel well, but leaves the skin clear and the pores unclogged.

What causes skin coloration?

Just like hair, the skin has a pigment that gives it its color. The sunlight reacts with this pigment and you can get a pretty tan. Sometimes the pigment is affected only in small areas; then instead of tanning, you freckle.

What causes blushing or blanching?

There are little muscles in the skin around the blood vessels that contract and expand. When they contract, the blood vessels become narrower and less blood flows through them. When there is less blood near the surface of the skin, the skin becomes whiter. If the muscles expand, the blood vessels grow wider and let more blood flow through. Then the skin blushes or reddens. You can see the blush much more distinctly on the neck and face than elsewhere, because the tiny blood vessels are closer to the surface of the skin here.

Facts about the skin

The skin can really be called a "mirror of the system." Its texture and color change with changes in bodily health.

Emotions are recorded by the skin:

a. when you are embarrassed, your skin may flush and become red (see page 35);

b. when you are frightened, your skin may become white;

c. anger and laughter wrinkles are recorded on the skin of your face.

Skin stretches when you gain weight and shrinks when you lose weight. It is elastic. As you grow older, you lose your elasticity.

5. The Skeleton and the Muscle System

If you could peel off the skin and fat from your body, you would expose the muscle system. There are hundreds of muscles. Each separate muscle, made up of many muscle cells, is wrapped in a sheath or coating, and functions as one unit. The muscles support the internal organs and help the body move.

A muscle contraction in some ways resembles the elastic movements of a metal spring. When the movement has stopped, the spring relaxes. So it is with the muscles. They must rest and relax periodically if they are to function properly. If you sit too long in an uncomfortable position, you will feel cramped and achy. Your muscles are telling you that they have been working too long and want to relax.

Muscles have many shapes and sizes, depending on where they are located and what job they have to perform. They are attached to bones by "tendons," which are tough, elastic-type bands of connective tissue. You can actually feel a tendon on your neck. This tendon is very evident if you watch a weight-lifter at work.

Some muscles are so tiny as to be almost thread-like—such as the one which is concerned with the working of the eyelids. Others, such as the "hamstring" muscles in the back of the thigh, are very broad and powerful.

Muscles work in pairs—because there must always be one muscle to oppose the other—one raises the finger—one lowers the finger.

There are two muscular systems: the "voluntary" and the "involuntary" systems. These names are self-explanatory. You con-

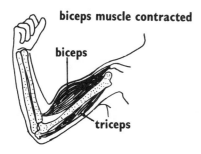

biceps muscle contracted

biceps

triceps

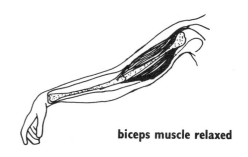

biceps muscle relaxed

sciously can control the muscles of the voluntary system. You can take a step or not. You can move your arm or let it lie still. But your involuntary muscular system functions whether or not you want it to do so. The heart, which is a muscle, pumps regularly without your being able to stop or start it. The muscles along the digestive tract move constantly without your conscious control.

Facts about muscles

It takes more muscles to frown than it does to smile.

There are more than 600 muscles in the human body.

Big, overdeveloped muscles are as bad as small, underdeveloped muscles. When a person's muscles are too big he becomes "muscle-bound." The big, over-developed muscles get in the way of the other muscles and keep them from functioning rapidly and smoothly.

Too strenuous muscle activity causes fatigue. The muscles actually lose some of their power because the body fuel supply runs down temporarily. After rest and proper nourishment they are ready to go.

"Charley horse" pain comes from unusual exertion of muscles where some of the tiny tendons and blood vessels are inflamed, and the pain may be felt for a few days until they heal.

The skeleton

The skeleton supports the body in very much the same way that the steel frame supports a building.

The skeleton, you can see, has two main parts:
1. The skull, spinal column and ribs.
2. The arms, legs, hips and shoulders.

There are 206 separate bones in the human body. Every newly-born infant has 206 bones and so does every adult. The bones differ only in size and strength.

Most of your bones are porous and hollow. Why? If the bones were solid, they would weigh so much that you could not move. Because they are porous, the bones are also more shock and blow resistant and more resilient.

You can see that the white, hard outside of a bone is porous (full of tiny openings). Ask a butcher for a piece of bone and look closely at it.

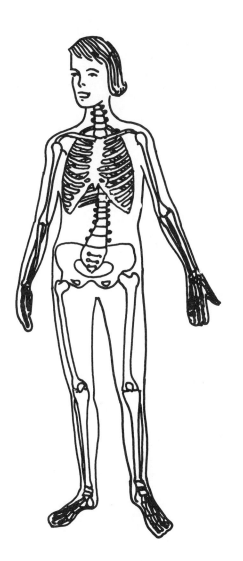

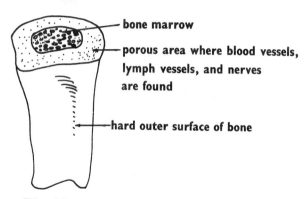

bone marrow

porous area where blood vessels,
lymph vessels, and nerves
are found

hard outer surface of bone

The blood vessels travel in and out of this outer part. It is made up mostly of a special balance or ratio of calcium and phosphorus in your diet. If this ratio is disturbed by improper diet, the bones grow too hard and brittle and may break easily; or they may grow too soft and bend.

The inside hollow of the bone, or bone marrow, has a twofold job. In some cases it is a "garage" for storing the necessary chemicals and fats the body needs; in other cases, it manufactures cells for the blood stream.

What happens when a bone breaks?

It is much like breaking off a branch from a tree. The broken edges are neither straight nor smooth, but jagged.

IRREGULAR BREAK IN A BONE

The first thing that happens after a bone breaks is that blood clots all around the break and "lymph" (see page 75) flows to the area.

#1—break in the bone

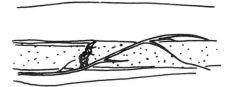

#2—bone cells moving towards each other from each side of the break

Next, each side of the break makes new bone cells and pushes them to the other. When they meet, the bone is healed.

#3—break has been closed

#4—calcium deposited around the break to make the area strong

Because the area where the break occurred is weak, the bone reinforces itself. It produces calcium around the broken edges so that in time the slight swelling of the calcium seals the weak spot completely. That area is now stronger than before the break, but less pliable.

Why should a break be set?

If the two edges of bone are not placed in the correct position, they may not meet properly. The bone would heal itself, but might heal crookedly or otherwise incorrectly. When a doctor sets a broken bone, he straightens the bone and places the two parts properly together.

SELF-KNIT BONE UNSET— MENDED INCORRECTLY　**BONE SET BY DOCTOR— MENDED CORRECTLY**

By putting a plaster cast or splint around the broken areas the bone is kept from moving and will heal together as it was set.

Although you can compare the skeleton to the steel frame of a building, there is one very important distinction. The building frame is kept from movement, but the human body must move. To make this movement possible, each bone is not welded to an adjacent bone but jointed much like a hinge on a wall and door. One joint that functions exactly like a hinge is the knee.

THE KNEE JOINT

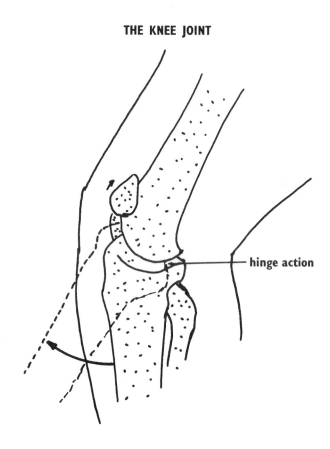

hinge action

It has movement in one direction only, just like a door, and cannot bend in the opposite direction without breaking the hinge or frame. This is necessary to keep the body in an upright position. There are other types of joints in the body. The elbow is a pivot-like joint. You can twist your forearm in almost any direction. ———→

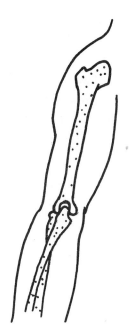

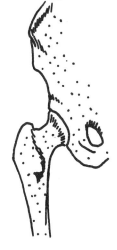

You also have a "ball-and-socket" joint in your hip and in your shoulder. ←———

Each of your 206 bones is joined to the next with a joint which permits whatever movement that bone needs. The spinal column is made up of a series of bones (called "vertebrae") with a cushion-like disc between. It is similar to a series of beads strung on a cord. ———→

The discs act as a sponge, absorb pressure and shock to the delicate bones which house the spinal cord.

To see what a spinal column looks like, you can go to your butcher shop and look at a chicken neck. Sometimes you can even find traces of the chicken's spinal cord.

The body has one very specialized kind of bone; this is the tooth. Teeth are somewhat different from other bones because they cannot heal themselves.

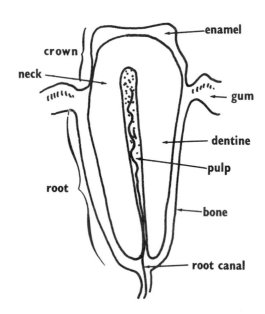

Look into your mouth; are all your teeth alike? No, they are not. Each tooth has a special, specific function.

Teeth buds are found in a baby before it is born. A young child has 20 baby or milk teeth. These are later pushed out by bigger, stronger adult teeth. This is necessary because the size of the jaw changes. An adult has 12 teeth more than a baby.

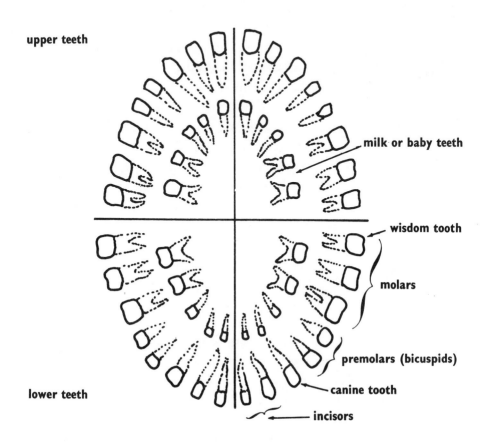

upper teeth

milk or baby teeth

wisdom tooth

molars

premolars (bicuspids)

canine tooth

lower teeth

incisors

What are the functions of teeth?

The front teeth are for biting or cutting; the back teeth or "molars" do the grinding or chewing. This is why the back teeth have much larger surfaces. Without the molars you could not chew your food properly or cut it up in small enough pieces to swallow comfortably. Try to chew with your front teeth. See how much longer it takes and how difficult it is.

What causes a cavity?

Food particles remaining in teeth invite bacteria to a feast. These bacteria attack the enamel of the tooth.

Acids in food can also attack and wear away enamel. When the enamel which protects the tooth is worn thin, bacteria break through the enamel and enter the soft part of the tooth. The result is a cavity. It is something like a little rust spot on a car. A speck of paint peels off and rust starts to attack the metal under the paint. Unless the rust is removed and new paint applied, the rust would wear away the metal and you would have a hole in your car.

Cavities are not the only thing that can be wrong with teeth. Sometimes teeth grow in the wrong way and you have what is called a "malocclusion," or in simpler words, an improper bite. These teeth can be moved to correct this condition. There are many ways to move teeth. Each involves a constant exerted pressure on the tooth in the direction you want it to go.

You can perform an experiment which is similar to teeth moving. All you need is a box, some sand, four pencils and some thin wire. Fill the box with sand about two inches deep, and wet the sand so it becomes slightly damp. Push the four pencils into the sand as far as they will go and attach the wire as shown in the diagram.

Pull the wire until the pencils make a 45-degree angle in the sand. The pencils will look like this:

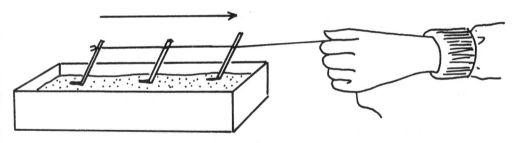

The pressure put on the sticks by pulling the string has moved them into a slanted position. After some time, the sand fills in the holes (like bones and gums in the mouth) and the sticks will stay slanted without the force of the string (brace).

In a few hours look and see what happened. There will be no space where the "roots" were. The damp sand will seep around the "roots," just like the bone and gum tissue do in the mouth.

This shows you what can be done for a simple malocclusion. Once the tooth is in the new position the bone and gum tissue will adjust to the new position and the tooth is held as fast and is as strong as it was before. Teeth which are properly positioned are apt to be healthier and last longer since the pressure placed on them by chewing will be even and not wear away the weak points in chewing. Look at the picture here. The malocclusion was corrected by the pressure of the wires exerted around the teeth, pushing them in the proper direction.

The picture at the top shows a wide separation between the two front teeth. Below, the dentist has added a wire brace which puts pressure on the two teeth. This pressure results in a movement of each tooth toward the other. When the work is completed, the space between the teeth is no longer there, because the teeth have moved toward each other.

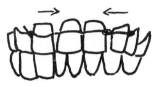

Facts about the skeleton

Babies very rarely break a bone, because an infant's bones are still soft. These bones bend very easily under pressure and straighten out when the pressure is gone. This is something like a reed: when the wind blows, the reed bends, but does not break.

As a person grows older, the bones become lighter in weight and more brittle, because calcium in the bones seeps out. That is why an older person may break a bone more easily than a younger one.

Do you know why bones tend to "creak" as you become older? The cartilage that covers the ends of the bone, cushioning the area where two bones meet, becomes thinner and sometimes disappears. Now bone meets bone, without a cushion in between and the joint stiffens and cracks.

The 22 bones that make up the skull do not move at all—with the exception of the "mandible" or lower jaw. This is hinged, so that it can move when you eat or talk.

6. The Digestive System

To the body, food is fuel to make it go. However, food cannot be used just as it is. It must be broken down into simple chemicals so that it can be absorbed by the cells of the body and give them the nourishment they need. This breaking down is done by the digestive tract or "alimentary canal," which is quite simply a chemical laboratory.

The alimentary canal consists of the mouth, œsophagus or gullet, stomach, small intestine and large intestine. The food travels along this canal and is acted on by various chemicals until all the food that can be used by the body is absorbed and the remainder, or waste material, is eliminated.

The first step is to break the food down into small pieces and wet it. The teeth begin the job

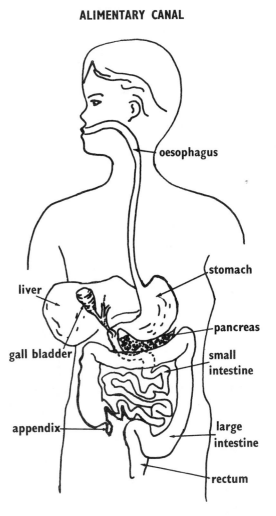

ALIMENTARY CANAL

oesophagus

stomach

liver

pancreas

gall bladder

small intestine

appendix

large intestine

rectum

by tearing the food into small pieces. After the teeth have ground the food to small size so that the chemicals can work properly, the first of the chemicals or reagents is added. This chemical comes from the salivary glands (which also wet the food) and acts to change starches to sugars.

You can perform this simple experiment at home. All you need are two plain crackers and some household iodine. First add a couple of drops of iodine to a small glass of water or if you have a test tube, to a test tube of water. This gives you a dilute iodine solution. Now take a cracker and wet it thoroughly with water. Place the wet cracker on a plate or piece of waxed paper. Add a few drops of your dilute iodine

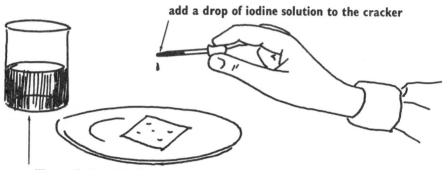

add a drop of iodine solution to the cracker

very dilute solution of iodine and water

solution. What happens? The bright purple color that you see is the positive test for starch.

Now, take a bite from the second cracker. Chew it thoroughly until it begins to taste sweet. Remove the chewed cracker from your mouth on to a plate or waxed paper and add a few drops of your dilute iodine solution. What happens? The fact that you no longer have the bright purple color shows you that the starch was changed to sugar.

As the food continues to pass down the alimentary canal, it is acted upon further. When it reaches the stomach, some of the food is temporarily stored; this is why the stomach is the widest section of the whole canal. There, also, further digestion takes place. Certain chemicals called "enzymes" are produced by the stomach to help break down food particles. The word "enzyme" comes from a Greek word which means "leavened."

Some of the food that has been acted upon by the enzymes is absorbed into the blood stream. The remaining food, only partly digested, goes further along, into the small intestine. To keep the food in the stomach long enough for certain digestive actions to take place, nature has placed a "door" at the end of the stomach. This door is called the "pylorus." This comes from a Greek word meaning "gate-keeper." The pylorus opens to let the digested food into the small intestine, where it becomes absorbed into the blood stream.

Semi-digested food also passes into the small intestine, where other enzymes work on the food to digest it completely. The section of the small intestine where these enzymes enter is called the "duodenum." This word comes from a Latin word meaning "twelve each." The twelve refers to the fingers, for the duodenum is about twelve fingers long.

The gall bladder which stores a fluid called "bile," made by the liver, opens into the duodenum. Bile helps break down fat particles. The "pancreas," a large gland, also opens into the duodenum and sends a mixture of chemicals, called "pancreatic juice," into the small intestine to further help digest food. By now, part of this food is already in a state that can be used by some of the cells. The cells in the walls of the small intestine absorb these tiny particles of nourishing chemicals and they enter in the blood stream.

How does the small intestine absorb some particles and not others? The small intestine absorbs like cheesecloth. Take a beaker or water glass, fill it with water and add ground blackboard chalk. You will get a milky fluid. Now when you pour this fluid through fine cheesecloth into a jar, the chalk is left behind in the cheesecloth, and the water in the jar is almost clear. The finer particles remain in solution and are almost completely dissolved.

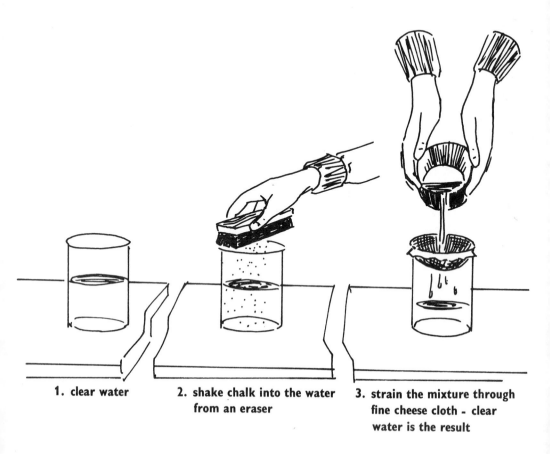

1. clear water

2. shake chalk into the water from an eraser

3. strain the mixture through fine cheese cloth - clear water is the result

From the small intestine, the food travels to the large intestine. The large intestine is not nearly as long as the small intestine, and as a result is not coiled up to save space. Rather it looks like an upside down capital U. That section which travels up, is called the "ascending colon."

The "appendix" is attached to the base of the ascending colon. It is simply a short hollow tube, sealed at the end. In lower forms of life, it was of use, but in modern man it is a vestigial organ. Vestigial simply means something that was fully developed or useful in an earlier stage of development.

Today it is important only because it can become inflamed and then cause trouble. Its removal by surgery causes no known change in the working of the body.

Then the large intestine or colon loops across the abdominal cavity. That portion is called the "transverse" colon. Finally it goes down and is called the "descending" colon. The lowest part of the descending colon is called the "rectum," and the rectum ends with an opening in the skin called the "anus."

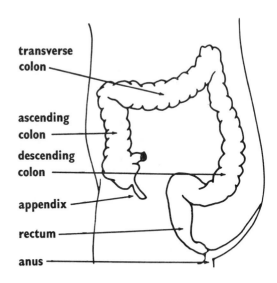

transverse colon

ascending colon

descending colon

appendix

rectum

anus

In the large intestine, water is removed, leaving the more solid material which cannot be used. It has not been "digested" and is finally removed as waste through the anus.

The anus is the opening of the rectum and is usually kept closed by a strong circular "sphincter" muscle. The word "sphincter" comes from a Greek word meaning "to shut tight." Today therefore the name refers to a muscle that controls the opening and closing of any tube or organ.

What keeps the food moving along this canal? Not the force of gravity, because you could eat and drink standing on your head. Actually it is a tiny pulsation of movements of the muscles all along the canal. These movements are called peristaltic waves. The word "peristaltic" comes from a Greek word meaning "clasping and compressing."

If you can visualize the wormlike wave motions as a series of hands, clasping and compressing a tube, you can picture the peristaltic waves.

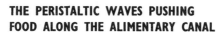

**THE PERISTALTIC WAVES PUSHING
FOOD ALONG THE ALIMENTARY CANAL**

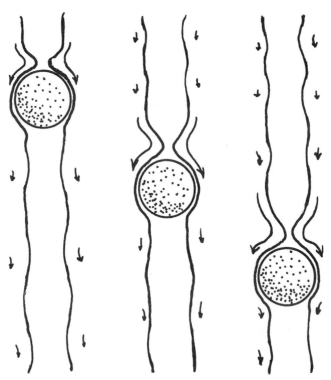

The now almost totally liquid nourishment goes in to the blood stream, which distributes it to the cells. What the cells can not use becomes liquid waste. The body removes this liquid waste in various ways. The lungs remove some of it. To see this, all you need is a mirror. Exhale on the mirror and you will see the liquid on the mirror's surface.

The skin removes some more of the waste in the form of perspiration and the major part of it is eliminated by the kidneys.

The kidneys act as filters, millions of tiny little filters working under high pressure. Once the waste is filtered out, the kidneys send back to the blood stream what is still usable, and the liquid waste is sent out to the bladder via two tubes called "ureters." In the bladder, the liquid (called "urine") is stored until there is enough urine for the body to eliminate. Then the sphincter muscle which keeps the bladder closed, opens, and the bladder discharges the urine into the "urethra" and out of the body through the urethral opening.

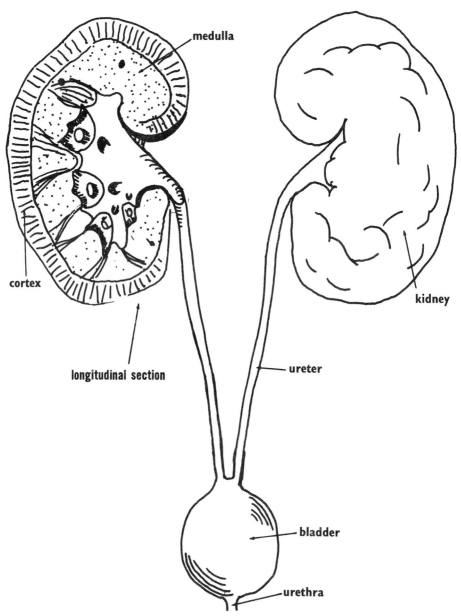

medulla

cortex

longitudinal section

kidney

ureter

bladder

urethra

200 litres of blood are filtered daily by the cortex and medulla of the kidneys. The waste is sent to the bladder; the usable material is sent back into the blood stream.

What actually causes these wastes? When the body breaks down chemical substances into smaller substances, heat is produced along with the material you want and the leftovers. The heat is used to keep the body warm. The smaller particles feed the cells and waste is removed. When you break down organic substances, of which all foods are composed, the final results are usually water and carbon dioxide. The carbon dioxide is a gas. What happens to this waste gas? It is removed from the body by the lungs and you exhale it.

Facts about digestion

All meat is almost completely digested by the enzymes and gases in the stomach, and goes directly into the blood stream.

Hunger pains can be caused by the empty stomach contracting and relaxing without having any food to "contract" on.

The small intestine has about 5,000,000 villi to increase the over-all area of it. A "villus" (from the Latin word which means "a tuft of hair") is a raised area, like a tiny finger, of the intestine walls and when greatly magnified looks like this:

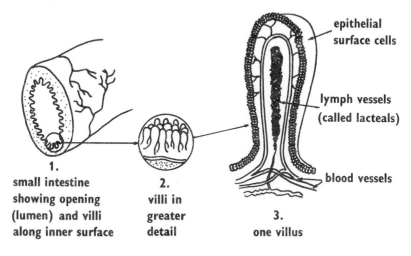

epithelial
surface cells

lymph vessels
(called lacteals)

blood vessels

1.
small intestine
showing opening
(lumen) and villi
along inner surface

2.
villi in
greater
detail

3.
one villus

In each villus there are blood vessels flowing through it so that the digested food may be absorbed. If you stretched out the small intestine completely, ironing out all the convolutions, or coils and folds, you would have an area more than five times the area of the skin surface. In an adult the small intestine is about 20 feet long.

In an adult the large intestine is about five feet long.

It takes about 24 hours for the food you eat to travel through the alimentary canal.

7. The Liver and the Spleen

The liver is the largest single organ in the body. This organ merits a chapter of its own, not because of its size, but because it does a great many important jobs. Not even the scientists know exactly how it performs all of its chores.

The liver lies in the upper right part of the body just under the ribs. It is very soft and spongy and the organs around it press into it. In an adult it weighs around three pounds. You can imagine the liver to be a huge building with a maze of crooked hallways and long narrow rooms. The rooms have no doors or ceilings but are openly connected with each other by walls. If you can imagine walls that are built, not out of stone, but of liver cells, only one cell thick, you can get a picture of this three-dimensional maze.

The liver has a strategic position in the body. It is close to the heart and receives the oxygen it needs to function from a small artery called the "hepatic artery." "Hepatic" comes from a Greek word meaning "liver." This artery runs directly from the largest artery leaving the heart, the "aorta." The blood leaves the liver through two large blood vessels, the "hepatic veins." The hepatic veins empty right into the "inferior Vena Cava," one of the widest veins, which goes directly into the heart. "*Vena Cava*" are two Latin words which mean "hollow vein."

The liver occupies this position because it is a filter and cleansing station that purifies the blood. It removes harmful materials and destroys body poisons and bacteria or inactivates them by chemical means. Most of the blood going into the liver, bringing these harmful

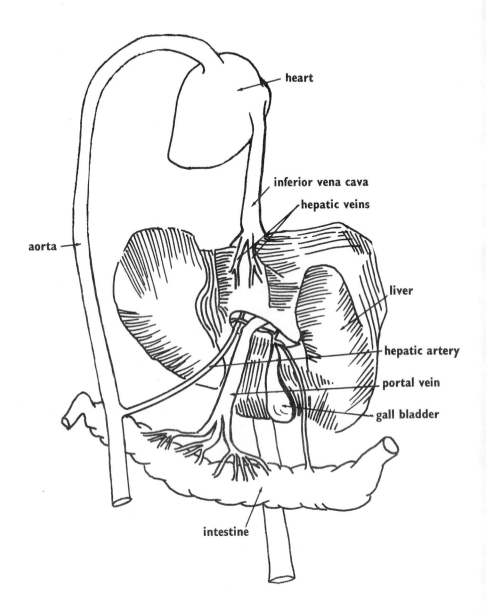

heart

inferior vena cava

hepatic veins

aorta

liver

hepatic artery

portal vein

gall bladder

intestine

LIVER

substances, comes from capillaries of the intestines. A vein from the spleen and a few veins from the stomach plus the capillaries from the intestines, flow together into one vein called the "portal" vein. It is called the portal vein because it goes right into the liver through an opening called the "door" of the liver.

Besides purifying the blood from the stomach, intestines and spleen, the liver has other jobs to do. It is a storage place for food, particularly sugars and fats which you need to give you energy and vitamins. The liver takes the sugars from the blood, and converts them into an inactive substance which it stores. When the body needs these sugars the liver changes them back to active sugars that the body can use, and sends them into the blood stream.*

Another job that the liver does is to destroy worn-out red blood cells. It breaks down the haemoglobin (an iron compound which holds oxygen in red blood cells) changing it into a reddish and greenish pigment which the body gets rid of through the intestines. Whatever parts of the red blood cells are still usable it sends out to be reused in the making of new red blood cells. The liver takes waste products such as "urea," a salt, and "uric acid" out of the blood and sends them into the intestines to be removed from the body with other waste material.

The liver makes bile, which is stored in the gall bladder. You have already learned that this bile helps aid digestion by breaking down fatty substances.

Filtering and cleaning the blood, storing energy-producing proteins and antibodies, removing wastes and aiding in digestion are just a few of the jobs the liver does. When you think about this, you will realize what an important part the liver plays in the day to day job of keeping your body living, growing and healthy.

---

* The liver also makes blood plasma, proteins, albumin, fibrinogen, prothrombin and antibodies. The fibrinogen and prothrombin are needed to help form blood clots. The antibodies counteract disease-producing poisons.

The spleen

The "spleen" is about the size of a fist. It is located below the diaphragm, just behind the stomach. It stores blood and sends it into the blood stream, when it is needed. The spleen also destroys worn-out red blood cells and sends into the body whatever material can be re-used in making new red blood cells.

Facts about the liver

The liver takes up about 1/50 of the total body weight.

It performs 70 different jobs.

The body can exist with $\frac{1}{2}$ of the brain healthy, only one lung, about $\frac{1}{2}$ of the stomach, $\frac{1}{2}$ the large intestine, and only 1 kidney. The body can function without adenoids, tonsils, gall bladder, spleen, or appendix, but the body *must* have at least 2/3 of the liver *intact* and *healthy* in order to survive.

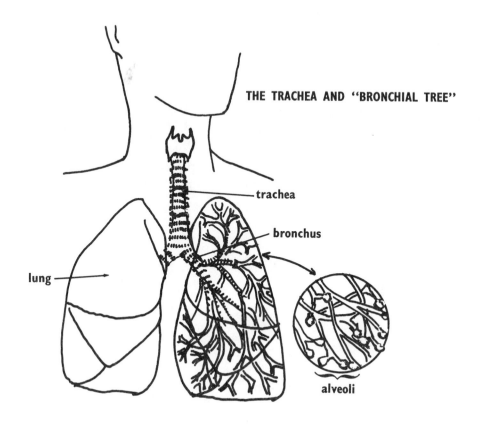

THE TRACHEA AND "BRONCHIAL TREE"

trachea

bronchus

lung

alveoli

8. The Respiratory System

What does the respiratory system do? It brings air, which is made up of a great percentage of oxygen, into the body and removes from the body carbon dioxide and waste gases. The cells need the oxygen from the air to help break down foods and supply energy. The carbon dioxide, the result of the breakdown of the foods, is sent out. Most of this carbon dioxide-oxygen exchange takes place in the lungs.

How does the air get into the lungs and how do the gases leave? The lungs lie in that part of the body called the "thorax," and the cavity around them is naturally called the "thoracic cavity." The bottom of the thoracic cavity is a muscular sheet called the "diaphragm." The sides of the thoracic cavity are partially made up by the ribs. As you breathe in, or inspire, the ribs go out slightly, and the diaphragm drops. Now you have a larger thoracic cavity, with less air pressure. To equalize the air pressure (otherwise you would collapse) air rushes into the lungs which fill up and increase in size. As the diaphragm relaxes (goes back into its original place) the space in the thoracic cavity decreases, and the lungs are forced to give up the gases in them so that once again the air pressure is equalized. This is called "expiration," or "exhaling," because now you expire or exhale the gases in the lungs. But the gases in the lungs are not the same as those you breathed in or inspired. The oxygen from the breathed-in air has been sent to the blood stream and the waste gases from the blood stream have been given to the lungs. This exchange is taking place constantly in the tiny air sacs that make up the greater portion of the lungs.

Now you see that when you breathe in and out you are not really enlarging your lungs or decreasing their size. The lungs are forced to inflate and deflate to keep the air pressure in the cavity equal. In some ways you can compare this action to a bellows. As you separate the sides of the bellows (drop of diaphragm, expansion of ribs), you are decreasing the air pressure in the bellows. Air flows into the bellows sacs (lungs) to equalize the pressure. When you squeeze the bellows sides together (diaphragm relaxes, ribs relax) you are increasing the pressure inside the bellows (thoracic cavity). The bellows sacs give up the air and they deflate.

How does the air that you breathe in get to the air sacs?

The air you breathe in through your nose passes through a filter system. All the cells lining the whole respiratory system have little hairs ("cilia"), which do the filtering. Besides being filtered, the air becomes heated. If you go out on an extremely cold day and take a quick deep breath, you will feel a sudden discomfort, but if you inhale slowly and give the air a chance to get warmed, this does not happen.

The air goes from the nasal cavity into the "trachea" or "windpipe." The windpipe is specially constructed to keep it from collapsing. It is made of a series of cartilage rings.

> If you put your fingers on your throat and run them up and down, you can feel the rings. From the trachea the air goes into the "bronchi"—tubes that extend out from the trachea. These bronchi separate into tiny branches after they reach the lungs.

At the end of these branches are little air sacs called "alveoli."* It is here that the gas exchange takes place. The little alveoli are surrounded by tiny little blood vessels called "capillaries." Here the oxygen leaves the lungs and goes into the blood vessels. At the same time there are little capillaries bringing the carbon dioxide, collected from the body, going to the alveoli. The gas leaves them and enters the air sacs. When you exhale, this carbon dioxide leaves by the same path as the oxygen entered.

You can now see how very important the respiratory tract is. Naturally, it is protected in many ways. When something accidentally enters the lungs, that is, foreign matter, you are forced to cough until you remove that foreign material.

* The trachea, bronchi, branches and alveoli resemble an upside-down tree, and are often called the "bronchial tree" for that reason.

Have you ever swallowed rapidly while eating, and suddenly had a coughing spell? You may say, "Oops, the food went down the wrong tube." What actually happens? In your throat the "œsophagus" or "gullet" lies next to the trachea. Both open into the throat. It would be very easy for food, instead of going into the œsophagus, to drop into the trachea. But nature does not let that happen. Lying against the upper part of the trachea is a little flap, or valve called the "epiglottis."

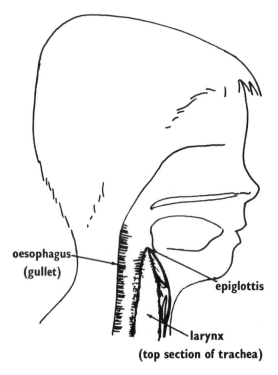

oesophagus (gullet)

epiglottis

larynx
(top section of trachea)

EPIGLOTTIS COVERING THE TRACHEA

When you swallow, the trachea moves upwards against the epiglottis, and no food can travel down the trachea. When you inhale, the trachea is not forced against the epiglottis, and the air can go down into the trachea. Sometimes, a small piece of food gets caught or some liquid flows down because the epiglottis does not come into contact with the trachea quickly enough. The food has started to go down "the wrong tube." Now you cough until the food particle is released and can go into the œsophagus.

Facts about respiration

Although you can consciously control the rate of your breathing you cannot stop long enough to suffocate. As soon as the carbon dioxide in the body builds up to a certain extent, a message is sent to the brain. The brain then takes over and forces you to breathe. If you should hold your breath too long, you will simply pass out. Once you are unconscious, you automatically start breathing again.

When you sleep in a room with closed doors and windows, you do not sleep well. Very little fresh air comes into the room, so that you do not get the needed amount of oxygen (O_2). You breathe out carbon dioxide (CO_2) which enters the room air. You breathe in the room air, already filled with the carbon dioxide you breathed out or expired. At the end of eight hours, you have a room filled with enough carbon dioxide to make you groggy and sleepy. But if you have an open window, fresh air laden with oxygen can readily enter the room and you are always receiving enough oxygen to keep your body refreshed.

It is unwise to sleep in a room with many green plants. Green plants also breathe. During the day, when it is light, plants take in carbon dioxide and give up or expire oxygen. At night, when it is dark, plants reverse the process and just as you do, they inhale oxygen and exhale carbon dioxide.

9. The Circulatory System

This system is composed of a group of organs which transport fluid from one part of the body to another. The fluid is blood and it feeds and waters the cells of the body. If you can imagine a canal network constantly filled with all kinds of cargo boats you can get some kind of picture of this system. However a pump is needed to keep this liquid moving and that is precisely what the heart does.

The heart is a muscle divided into four separate chambers, each divided by a muscle wall and valves. As these chambers contract and relax they force the blood in and out of the heart. There are valves which open and close between the four chambers. The relaxation and contraction of the chambers and the opening and closing of the valves cause the sounds your doctor listens to through a stethoscope.

In an infant, the heartbeat is much faster than in an adult.

68

THE HEART

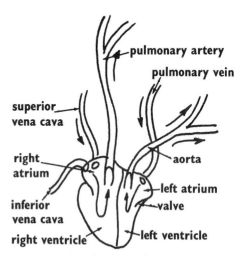

All the blood flowing into the heart comes from veins from all parts of the body except from the lungs, and enters the right side of the heart. The heart pumps that blood to the lungs via the pulmonary arteries. In the lungs the blood gets its oxygen and goes back to the left side of the heart, via the pulmonary veins. From there the heart pumps this blood to all the arteries of the body via the strongest artery, the aorta.

It beats about 140 times a minute, compared to 72 times a minute for an adult. That is why, when you catch a small bird or animal and hold it, you might think it is frightened because its heart is beating so fast. This is not true. The smaller the being, the faster the heartbeat.

You can try a small experiment yourself to see how the heart works. All you need is a small basin and water.

Cup your hands like those in the diagram, squeeze together and watch the water squirt out. When you relax, the water enters your hands again. Keep this up for a while and see how rapidly your hands become tired. Now just imagine how much work the heart does. It pumps on the average 700,000 cubic inches of blood a day for your entire life.

For what does a doctor listen when he listens to your heart?

1. Primarily to hear that the valves or doors to the heart chambers are opening and closing properly.

2. That there is no blood leakage between beats.

3. That there is no opening in the muscle walls which is letting blood seep through.

He hears all this in the "Lub'dub, Lub'dub" sound your heart makes.

You can listen to this without a real stethoscope. All you need is a cardboard tube (from a roll of bathroom tissue) to concentrate the sound waves, and another person. Find the heart, press the tube against it, place your ear against the other end of the tube and you can hear the beating rhythm of the human heart. Or you can make your own simple stethoscope by using a piece of rubber tubing and an ordinary kitchen funnel.

It is the contracting and re-laxing of the chamber that causes the blood leaving the heart to move in spurts. Whenever an artery is near the surface of the skin you can actually feel the spurts. This is what a doctor does when he "takes your pulse." You can take your own pulse using your second or third finger. (Do not use the thumb because the thumb's own pulse beat will interfere.) You can go one step further and see that your blood spurts, rather than flows. To see the movement, you will need some chewing gum and a tooth-pick. First find your pulse, put

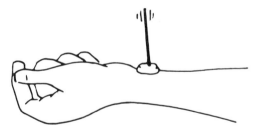

the gum on it, insert the tooth-pick and watch it move. You can even count these movements.

You can try another experiment with these materials. After you have counted how often your heart beats while you are resting, remove the gum and toothpick and jump up and down ten times. Now replace the gum and toothpick. See how much faster your heart beats after exercise.

The fluid that the pump moves is not really red in color; it just looks red because of one type of little boat sailing in it, namely, the "red blood cell." These little cells—under a

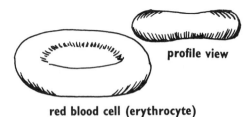

red blood cell (erythrocyte)

microscope—look like a dough-nut or a life-preserver, but they have a thin layer of cells covering the hole.

The red blood cell is called an "erythrocyte" and the erythro-cyte contains haemoglobin, which combines with oxygen. This is how oxygen is distributed through the system. The word

white blood cell (leukocytes)

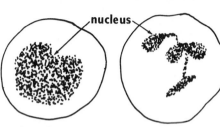

| lymphocyte (one type of white blood cell) | neutrophil this form of white blood cell makes up 65-75% of the average white blood cell count in the body |

"erythrocyte" comes from a Greek word which means "red."

Another boat in the canal is the "white blood cell." The white cells are called "leuco-cytes" or "phagocytes." The word "phagocyte" means "cell eater" and comes from a Greek word which means eating.

71

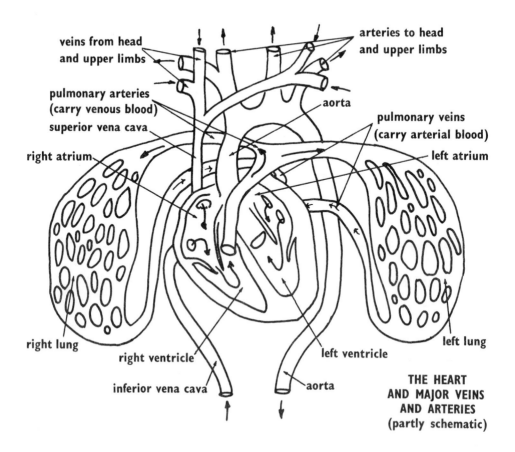

veins from head and upper limbs

arteries to head and upper limbs

pulmonary arteries (carry venous blood)

aorta

superior vena cava

pulmonary veins (carry arterial blood)

right atrium

left atrium

right lung

left lung

right ventricle

left ventricle

inferior vena cava

aorta

THE HEART
AND MAJOR VEINS
AND ARTERIES
(partly schematic)

These white cells are the soldiers in our bodies and attack the invaders. When a germ enters, they march like armies towards it, engulf it and destroy it. The nourishment or food that has been broken down in the chemical factory or digestive system also travels in the blood stream.

While this canal network is very well organized, there are only two directions in which it travels, and each is one way only. There are canal systems leaving the heart (arteries) that go to all parts of the body; there are canal systems that go from the body to the heart (veins) and there are tiny little U-turns—the "capillaries."

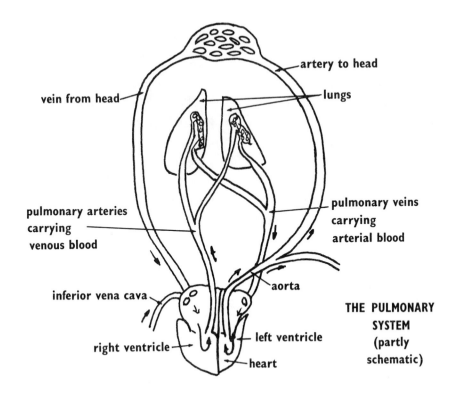

artery to head

vein from head

lungs

pulmonary arteries
carrying
venous blood

pulmonary veins
carrying
arterial blood

inferior vena cava

aorta

THE PULMONARY
SYSTEM
(partly
schematic)

right ventricle

left ventricle

heart

The arteries carry the rich oxygen-charged blood and food to the various parts of the body; the veins take the blood from which the cells have removed their cargo and given up wastes back to the heart. Naturally the arteries must pick up the oxygen somewhere and this is where a slight deviation occurs.

There is within the circulatory system a self-enclosed system called the "pulmonary" system, whose sole function is to take the blood from the heart and give it oxygen in return for the carbon dioxide picked up by the veins. Since you have already read that the exchange of these gases takes place in the lungs, it must be obvious to you that the pulmonary system involves the heart and the lungs only.

In this system there is only one port of call. The waste material, accumulated in the form of gaseous carbon dioxide and some traces of water, travels from the heart in the pulmonary artery to the lungs and oxygen is taken on. Then the pulmonary vein, loaded with oxygen, goes back into the heart from which it is pumped into the main arterial canal called the "aorta." There it begins its travels throughout the body. This is the only time that an artery carries blood filled with wastes and a vein carries blood filled with oxygen.

From the aorta, arteries branch off and go to each and every one of the organs of the body, giving oxygen and food to all the hungry cells. Wherever an artery goes to an organ, a vein leaves it, taking from the cells all the waste and unused materials. These two systems, the venous and the arterial, parallel each other, just like cargo routes. One route goes to a port of call with a specific cargo; in the arterial system that cargo is food and oxygen. Then another route leaves that port of call taking an empty boat or a boat filled with cargo received at that port. In the venous system the boats leave with waste products.

Since all your blood vessels are connected, why is it when you cut yourself you don't bleed to death? To prevent this, the blood clots. What causes a clot? It is caused by yet another "boat," "fibrinogen."

The fibrinogen forms an actual web, which keeps liquid from flowing out. The web becomes denser and dries to form a "plug." This plug or scab remains until the cut is healed.

Sometimes, however, a cut or tear in a vein or artery is so large that the body cannot heal it in time. Then the doctor must help by bringing the torn or cut edges together and holding them by sewing or taping until the healing has taken place.

What else does the blood do? Besides all the previously mentioned boats it also carries antibodies. These little soldiers help the white cells fight disease and illness. The liquid that carries all these boats is actually colorless and as it travels through the tiny capillaries some of the liquid leaks out. Most of the boats are too large to seep out with it; it just carries the minutest amount of cargo, mostly in the form of nourishment or food. Then it flows freely among the cells feeding and wetting them. Because it is no longer confined or contained within the specific canal network of veins and arteries it is not now called blood or serum but "lymph," from the Latin word meaning "water."

The lymph is not moved along by the heart beat so it must get pushed around another way. It moves as you do. Whenever you move, muscles begin to contract and relax. This force moves the lymph along. The lymph also picks up waste material from the cells it feeds and eventually enters the lymph vessels and finally the lymph "nodes." These nodes are filter systems. They filter the waste from the lymph and destroy the waste.

One very common lymph node is a tonsil; another is the adenoid. The adenoids lie at the back of the mouth and up slightly. The tonsils lie somewhat lower down in the throat. These lymph nodes trap any infectious material that enters the nose when you breathe. Finally, the lymph, relieved of all its cargo of wastes, seeps back into the veins again to start its journey all over again.

Sometimes when you feel tired and sluggish but not really sleepy, you may have a sudden urge to run around. All at once you realize you feel wide awake. What has actually happened? The lymph filled with collected waste material, did no travelling because you did no moving. Suddenly you moved quite a bit, forcing the lymph into the nodes where it was filtered of its waste. From the nodes the waste material was sent out of your system. You literally washed your body internally.

This is just one of the many reasons why some form of exercise is good for you and why it becomes very tiresome to sit or lie still for long periods of time.

Facts about circulation

250,000,000 cells in the blood are destroyed and replaced daily.

All the liquid within the human body (and the body is more than 70% water) passes through the blood.

Under normal conditions there are 500 times as many red blood cells as white blood cells.

The red blood cells are manufactured by the bone marrow.

As do all cells these red blood cells have a nucleus. However, once these cells leave the bone marrow, the nucleus disappears (perhaps that causes the slight dent in their surface).

Once in the blood these red blood cells can no longer truly be called cells but merely containers to carry the haemoglobin.

The white cells are made in the spleen. When infection strikes the body, many more of these cells are made to engulf and isolate the invaders.

That is why so often a blood count is taken when you are ill.

The entire over-all length of the veins, arteries and capillaries is about 12,000 miles.

10. The Central Nervous System

The central nervous system is like a combination policeman, switchboard and electronic calculator. It has two main parts:

1. The central system, which includes the brain and the spinal cord.

2. The peripheral system, which includes the nerves which come from the spinal cord and base of the brain to the different parts of the body.

The nervous system is made up of nerve cells called "neurons." The neurons are different from any other cell. They have "feelers" attached which are similar to electric wires, and impulses or messages can jump across these wires from one cell to another. The "feelers" of these neurons vary in size. Impulses going to the neuron travel along the feeler called "dendrite." Impulses leaving the neuron travel along the feeler called the "axon." All impulses must go through at least one of these two switchboards, the brain or the spinal cord. From the switchboard the impulses are sent out to the neurons along the axons and dendrites.

The brain in an average adult weighs about three pounds. Compare this with some of the simpler electronic computers which weigh many tons.

The brain has three main parts. The "cerebrum"—which is what you would see if you were looking directly down on a person with an open skull—the "cerebellum" and the "medulla oblongata," which

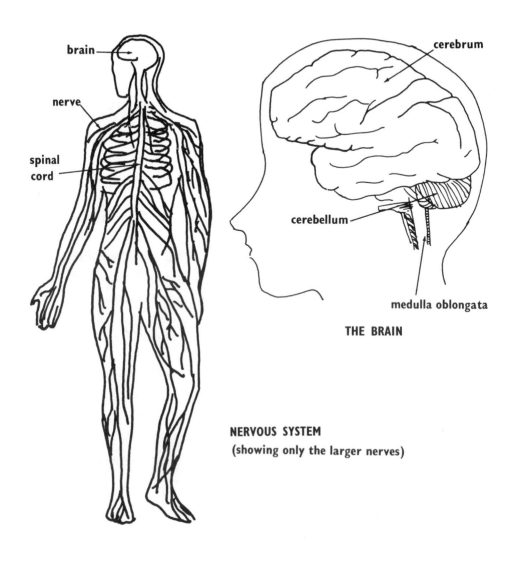

brain

nerve

spinal
cord

cerebrum

cerebellum

medulla oblongata

THE BRAIN

NERVOUS SYSTEM
(showing only the larger nerves)

connects directly with the spinal cord. The brain has specific areas which control specific activities, such as appetite, memory and emotions, and movement.

Unlike the skin and other tissue that can heal itself, nervous tissue

78

cannot. Once some nerves are cut or destroyed by disease, those nerves are dead and the function they control stops. Luckily, one uses only a small percentage of the brain and in some cases other areas can be taught to take over the function of that part that was destroyed.

Because the brain and spinal cord are so delicate, they are both housed in areas which give them special protection. The brain is covered by a liquid to absorb shock, a membrane (pliable lining) and finally by the skull, which consists of hard resilient bone.

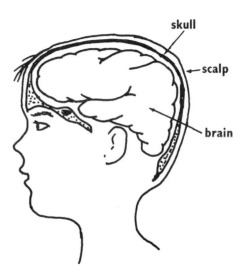

The brain is protected by the skull and by the liquid between two membranes, one covering the brain and the second separated by the liquid. Then still a third tough membrane covers the other two, and finally the skull covers all three.

It is as well, if not better, protected than the most fragile electronic equipment, so that it does not become jarred or crushed.

You can see some of this protection in a baby under one year old. The skull has not fully fused or grown together and there is a spot on the top of the head where there is no bone. You can actually feel the tough membrane just under the skin. Once the bones of the skull have grown together, they are stronger than non-fused bones. It takes quite a blow or fall to injure the brain.

The spinal cord is also well protected by the spinal column. (See illustration on page 43.) The spinal cord is not a single string. It is made up of many nerve fibres, like an electric cable covered by a sheath.

Coming out of the brain are twelve pairs of nerves which connect directly with the eyes, nose, ears, lungs, heart and digestive system. Coming out of the spinal cord are 31 pairs of nerves which connect with other parts of the body. These 43 pairs of nerves make up the peripheral system. How do they work? Take for an example, walking. Without realizing it, because by now it has become automatic, you phone a message to the main switchboard, the brain, that you want to take a step. The switchboard then relays the message directly to the nerves of the parts of the body to be used. Your knee must bend, your foot must go off the ground and your balance be shifted.

All this is done in a smooth rhythm that comes from practice. The switchboard has received that message so often it sends, without hesitation, the right number of messages to the right number of places. Now take, for example, a baby just learning to walk. This is an entirely different matter. The message is the same but not having done it so often, the brain sends the signals more slowly. The proper areas must receive the signals correctly. The result is a clumsy walk that often ends in a fall.

How long does it take you to take one step? Less than one second. In that time the message has gone to the brain, been analyzed, and the correct series of actions telegraphed to the nerves in the proper areas. The muscles respond and the step is taken. All this, in less than a second, without your really being aware of how involved the command is which you have ordered. Very efficient!

Yet there are times when the body must be even more efficient. Often there is not even that much time to spare before acting. When this happens, it is called a "reflex action" and usually the main switchboard, the brain, is bypassed to save time. If you accidentally touch a red-hot stove or a candle flame, the nerve endings in your fingertips send the message to the spinal cord which immediately sends the message back to the arm to pull away.

There is just not enough time to analyze the message, send it to the brain and have the brain send back instructions. Before you really know what you are doing, you have pulled your hand away. In this fraction of a second you may have saved yourself from seriously burning your hand.

Another set of nerves takes care of action or motion that must be done to keep you alive and must therefore be done automatically. Air must be pumped in and out of the lungs, food must be digested and absorbed and the heart must keep on pumping. These nerves make up the "autonomic nervous system." The word "autonomic" comes from two little Greek words, *autos*, which means "self" and *nomos*, which means "law." In anatomy the word means "acting without conscious desire." The whole autonomic system is self-governing and acts independently of the conscious mind.

Facts about the nervous system

Outgoing impulses can travel along the axons at a speed as high as 200 miles per hour.

A person can live with only half of his brain functioning. The great scientist, Pasteur, suffered from a brain haemorrhage and was slightly paralyzed on one side. It was only after his death that doctors discovered that 50 per cent of his brain had been injured by that haemorrhage.

Nerve cells can be stimulated by outside currents, such as those obtained from an ordinary dry cell.

When the current flows, the nerve reacts. When it ceases, the nerve impulses stop. To prove this, wires can be attached to the motor nerves of a dead frog leg and to a dry cell. When the circuit is completed, the impulses along the frog's nerves cause the leg muscle to contract, and the leg actually kicks. When the current is broken, the leg is still.

11. The Gland System

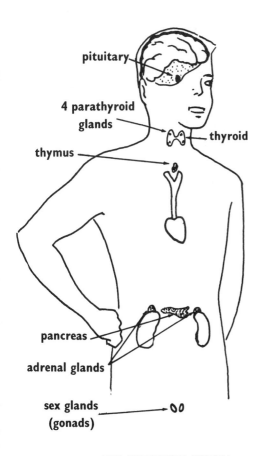

pituitary

4 parathyroid glands

thymus

thyroid

pancreas

adrenal glands

sex glands (gonads)

THE ENDOCRINE SYSTEM

The glands in the body manufacture chemical substances called "hormones." The word hormone comes from a Greek word meaning "to excite" and that is what hormones do. They excite or stimulate various parts of the body to function properly. Some glands send these hormones directly into the blood stream and so are called "ductless" or "endocrine" glands. The other type, like the pancreas, have little tubes or ducts through which they send out the hormones and therefore are called "duct" glands.

To keep the body working normally, these glands must be regulated so that just the right number of hormones are released. The "pituitary" gland, located in the brain, is the most important gland.

83

Besides making hormones, the pituitary directs and controls all the other glands such as the "thyroid," "parathyroid," "adrenal" glands, etc.

For example, consider the thyroid gland. It produces "thyroxin," which is needed for proper body growth and mental development. The thyroid gland sends out thyroxin to protect the body against abnormal mental and physical development.

All the hormones together regulate digestion and the changing of the food you eat into useful nourishment needed to rebuild cells—a process called "metabolism." The hormones also regulate physical maturity, reproduction, and some mental ability.

12. The Reproductive System

The reproductive organs

The ability to reproduce their own kind separates living things, such as plants and animals, from non-living things, such as water and rocks. In human beings, a new person is produced by the sexual union of a male and a female. A baby, at birth, is made up of millions of separate cells. All the cells in his or her body come from just two special cells. These cells are called the "ovum" or "egg cell" and the "sperm cell."

You were in two separate places before these two cells met to finally make you *you*. One half of you was in your mother, in her ovum; and the other half was in your father, in his sperm cell. There are many advantages in starting life from two separate cells. In this way, a baby inherits characteristics from two people. This allows for an unimaginable number of different characteristics.

Let us look at these two mysterious life-giving cells. The egg cell or ovum is the largest cell produced in the human body. It can just barely be seen with the naked eye. It is almost perfectly round in shape.

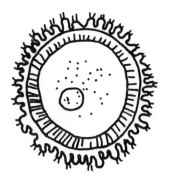

egg cell or ovum

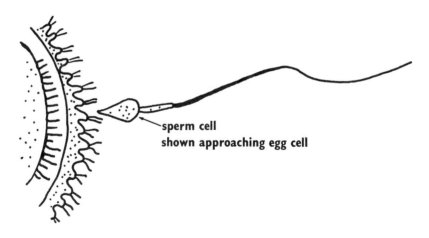

**sperm cell
shown approaching egg cell**

The male sperm cell, on the other hand, is very, very tiny. Many thousands would fit on the head of a pin and you need a microscope to see one of them. The male sperm cell is shaped quite differently from the ovum, for it resembles a tadpole. It has a small head that is somewhat flat and pointed at the top, and a long thin tail about ten times as long as the head. The tail gives the sperm mobility, and it can move or rather swim very rapidly. It is this mobility, or swimming ability, that makes it possible for the sperm cell to unite with the egg.

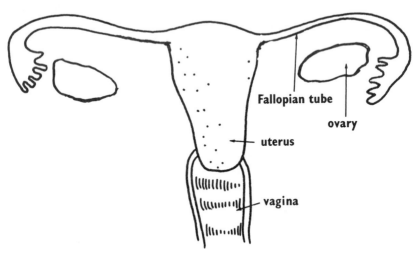

Fallopian tube

ovary

uterus

vagina

When a baby girl is born, she already has many special cells in her body, which become egg cells when she matures. While the girl is still young, until she reaches puberty (this word comes from a Latin word meaning "adult"), these special cells do not function and are not yet ready to start their part in creating a new life. They are kept in two sac-like organs called "ovaries," one on each side of the body.

As a girl matures, many changes take place in her body. One of them is the maturing of these egg cells. When she reaches puberty, the first mature egg cell breaks loose from the ovary and begins its trip through her body. Lying close to the ovary on each side is a narrow tube called the "Fallopian tube." When the mature egg is released from the ovary it goes into the Fallopian tube through an opening in the tube that looks as if it had small fingers around it.

These fingers seem to suck up the ovum into the Fallopian tube. The egg travels through the tube and drops into the "uterus" or "womb" into which the Fallopian tube opens. The uterus is a hollow, pear-shaped organ with very muscular walls. Each month, as an egg cell leaves the ovary, the uterus develops a thick lining. The lining becomes thick and has a blood supply in it so that if a fertilized egg were to enter it, it could provide the nourishment needed for that fertilized egg.

When the egg that enters the uterus is not fertilized it cannot develop, and the thick lining and extra blood supply are not needed. The uterus then discharges the unfertilized egg, the lining and the extra blood supply. This discharged matter becomes the menstrual flow that every girl experiences monthly from puberty on. It is composed of the cells that made up the extra thickness of the uterus wall, the unfertilized egg and the extra blood supply, and it passes from the uterus into the "vagina," a tube that opens out of the body, between the anus and the urethra.

The menstrual flow is only one of the signs of puberty in a girl.

Besides these internal developments, there are also more obvious external signs that the young girl is growing into a woman. Her body loses its immature muscular appearance and takes on a softer and more rounded one. The breasts develop and the hips curve out. Hair appears under the arms and around the external sex organs.

While all this maturing goes on in the girl what happens to the boy? As egg cells are formed in the ovaries of the girl, so sperm cells are formed in two organs called "testes." The ovaries are inside the girl's body, but the sperm cells inside the testes are outside the male in a sac called the "scrotum." The scrotum lies behind the external male sex organ, the "penis." When a boy reaches puberty the sperm cells grow in large numbers in the testes. The sperms are not released once a month like egg cells but are stored. When they leave the body they pass from the testes into a tube, where a fluid called "semen" has been produced. The sperms swim in this fluid into a small pouch called the "seminal vesicle" and remain here until they flow out of the body from the "urethra," which, in the boy, opens out at the tip of the penis.

In the boy, as in the girl, there are outward changes that can be seen as the boy matures. He too develops hair under the arms and around the external sex organs. His body grows more muscular, his chest expands and his hips become narrower. At this time also his voice changes. It becomes deeper and more masculine.

Both boys and girls, when they reach puberty, have still another change in common. The sweat glands become more active, and more wastes are excreted. This greater amount carries with it a rather unpleasant aroma not found in undeveloped children. Therefore even greater care than before must be given to personal cleanliness.

Finally, when boys and girls reach puberty, they find an interest in each other, or an awareness of the other sex. Nature is making sure that the race of man will continue.

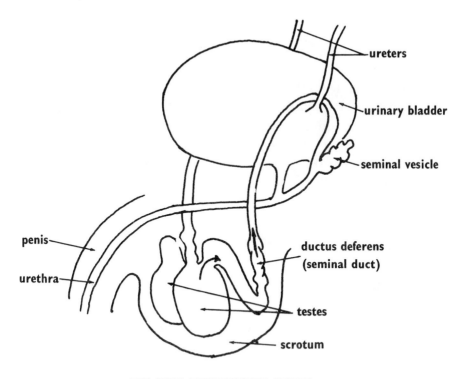

ureters

urinary bladder

seminal vesicle

penis

ductus deferens
(seminal duct)

urethra

testes

scrotum

THE MALE REPRODUCTIVE SYSTEM

Reproduction

Earlier, you read that the sex cells are very special cells. It takes one male and one female sex cell to form the beginning of a new life. But these cells are special for another reason. In the nucleus of each body cell are tiny microscopic structures called "chromosomes." These chromosomes contain the "genes." Genes decide the color of your hair, your eyes, your physical structure and even, to some extent, your personality. Every human cell has 46 chromosomes. Other species have cells with a greater or lesser number of chromosomes. The cells of horses each have 60 chromosomes. The cells of fruit flies have eight.

The only cells in the human body which do not have 46 chromosomes are the egg cells and the sperm cells. They have only 23 each. They are not complete cells, but only become complete when a sperm cell joins an egg cell. When this happens, a fertilized egg cell has been formed, complete with 46 chromosomes—23 from the sperm cell and 23 from the egg cell. As soon as the two cells unite, life begins.

What happens to the fertilized egg? It becomes attached to the thickened lining of the uterus and begins to divide. First, there are two cells, then four cells, eight cells, 16 cells and so on, until there is a small ball of millions of cells.

**THE FERTILIZED EGG DIVIDING AND
SUBDIVIDING IN THE EARLIEST STAGES**

Groups of cells now start to take specific shape and to function. One series becomes the bone cells of the developing baby, another series the skin cells, another the nerve cells, and so on, until after a period of a few months the baby becomes recognizable in shape.

The unborn baby develops and grows. It obtains food and oxygen from its mother through her blood stream. From the navel area of the baby a cord extends to the lining of the mother's uterus—the "umbilical cord." This cord contains blood vessels through which nourishment and oxygen travel to the baby. Once the baby becomes fully developed and able to live outside the mother, a period of time taking nine months, it is ready for birth. It leaves the uterus, travels down the vaginal canal and arrives through the opening called the vagina. At birth, the umbilical cord is cut by the doctor and now the baby must breathe and eat by itself. An entirely new life has begun.

INDEX

Ovum, 85

Pancreas, 49, 51, 83
Pancreatic juice, 51
Papilla, 14
Parathyroid glands, 83, 84
Penis, 88, 89
Perception, depth, 22
Peripheral system, 77, 80
Peristaltic waves, 53, 54
Perspiration, 34, 35, 55
Phagocytes, 71
Pigment, hair, 16
  skin, 35
Pituitary gland, 83, 84
Plasma, blood, 61
Pores, skin, 34
Portal vein, 60, 61
Premolars, 45
Prothrombin 61
Puberty, 87, 88
Pulmonary arteries, 68, 72ff.
  system, 73
  veins, 68, 72ff.
Pulse, 70
Pupil, 20, 21
Pylorus, 51

Rectum, 49, 53
Red blood cells, 11,
  61ff., 71, 76
Reproduction, 84, 85, 89
Reproductive organs, 85
  system, 85
  system, male, 89
Respiration, 67
Respiratory system, 63
Retina, 20, 21
Rods, 21, 23
Root, hair, 14, 33
Salivary glands, 50
Scab, 74
Scalp, 79
Sclera, 20
Scrotum, 88, 89
Seeing, 22, 23
Semen, 88
Semi-circular canals, 25,
  27, 28
Seminal duct, 89
  vesicle, 88, 89
Sense organs, 20

Setting bone break, 41
Sex cells, 89
  glands, 83
Shaft, hair, 14
Sickness, motion, 28
Sinuses, 30
Skeleton, 39
  and muscle system, 37
  facts, 48
Skin, a sense organ, 31
  cells, 90
  coloration, 35
  cross-section, 33
  facts, 34, 36
  pigment, 35
  pores, 34
Skull, 79, 80
Small intestine, 49ff., 57, 58
Sound waves, 24
Sperm cells, 85, 86, 88, 90
Sphincter muscle, 53, 55
Spinal column, 80
  cord, 77ff.
Spleen, 59, 61, 62, 76
Stapes, 26
Stethoscope, 69
Stirrup, 25, 26
Stomach, 49ff., 62
Straight hair, 17
Structure, cell, 9
Superior vena cava, 68, 72
Sweat glands, 33, 88
System, arterial, 74
  autonomic nervous, 81, 82
  endocrine, 83
  gland, 83
  male reproductive, 89
  nervous, 77, 78
  peripheral, 77, 80
  pulmonary, 73
  venous, 74

Tanning, 35
Taste buds, 31
Tear fluid, 24, 30
Teeth, 44, 45
Tendons, 37
Testes, 88, 89
Thorax, 64
Three-dimensional
  vision, 22
Thymus gland, 83

Thyroid gland, 83, 84
Thyroxin, 84
Tissue, blood, 10
  connective, 10, 37
  epithelial, 10
  gland, 10
  muscle, 10
  nervous, 10
Toenails, 18, 19
Tongue, 31
Tonsils, 62, 75
Trachea, 63, 65, 66
Transverse colon, 53
Triceps muscle, 38
Tube, Eustachian, 25
  Fallopian, 86, 87

Ultrasonic waves, 29
Umbilical cord, 90
Unfertilized egg, 87
Urea, 61
Ureters, 55, 56, 89
Urethra, 55, 56, 87ff.
Uric acid, 61
Urine, 55
Uterus, 86, 87, 90

Vagina, 86, 87, 90
Valve, 68
Vein, portal, 60, 61
Venous blood, 72, 73
  system, 74
Veins and arteries, 72ff.
Veins, hepatic, 59, 60
  pulmonary, 68, 72ff.
Ventricles, 68, 72, 73
Vertebrae, 43
Vesicle, seminal, 89
Vessels, blood, 58, 59, 65, 74
  lymph, 57
Villus, 57, 58
Vision (3-D), 22
Vitreus, 20
Voluntary muscular
  system, 37, 38

Wastes, 88
Waves, peristaltic, 53, 54
  ultrasonic, 29
White blood cells, 71, 76
Windpipe, 65
Wisdom teeth, 45